# Copyright

KDP Independent Publishing Platform

ISBN-13: 978-1091663510 (KDP-Assigned)

The content in this book meets the public domain requirements.
Differentiated works are unique illustrations.

*This Metamorphosis 1 & 2 book by Philip Glass is a method of learning featuring unique color-coded illustrations of sheet music.*
*Play Piano by Letters translates musical notation by replacing note symbols with letters.*

Visit www.PlayPianoByLetters.com to see more Piano Tabs.

Subscribe to our YouTube channel for new videos.

PlayPianoByLetters.com            YouTube Channel

# How to Read Piano Tab

This method of piano tab takes the note symbols out of sheet music and replaces them with letters.

- You read letters starting at the top and moving to the bottom of the page.

- A keyboard template is used as a guide, visible at the top of each page.

- Middle "C" is colored red or blue in the keyboard template header for easy reference on where to start the song.

- The rhythm count or beat is located in the left column along with each measure number and chords if needed.

- Notes played with the left hand are colored blue.

- Notes played with the right hand are colored red.

- As needed, fingering numbers are next to the note letters.

- When 2 or more notes are written horizontally, they are played together, indicated by a dotted line.

- A blue or red bold vertical line under a note letter represents a sustained count.

- A black "X" under a note letter represents a rest.

# Contents

# Metamorphosis One

## *Philip Glass*

*(Page 1 of 12)*

*Tablature by Joe Caligiuri*

Left Hand      Right Hand

| M e a s u r e | | Time: 4/4 |
|---|---|---|
| | | Tempo: 110 |
| | | Key: Am |
| | | Chord |

Beat

Keyboard labels: E F G A B C D E F G A B C D E F G A B C D E F G A B C

**Measure 1 — Em**
- Beat 1: E (4) · · G (2) · · B (1) · · · E (1) · · G (2) · · B (4)
- Beat 2: E · · · · G · · · · B · · · · E · · · · G · · · · B

**Measure 2 — G**
- Beat 1: D (5) · · · · · · G (2) · · B (1) · · D (1) · · · · · · G (2) · · B (4)
- Beat 2: D · · · · · · · · G · · · · B · · · · D · · · · · · · · G · · · · B

**Measure 3 — C7**
- Beat 1: C (5) · · · · · · · · G (2) · · B C (1) · · · · · · · · G (2) · · B (4)
- Beat 2: C · · · · · · · · · · G · · · · B C · · · · · · · · · · G · · · · B

**Measure 4 — C 13**
- Beat 1: C (5) · · E (3) · · · · · · Bb (1) · · C (1) · · E (2) · · · Bb (5)
- Beat 2: C · · · · E · · · · · · Bb · · C · · E · · · · · · · · · Bb

**Measure 5**
- Beat 4: X    X   X     X    X    X     X

**Measure 6 — Em**
- Beat 1: E (4) · · G (2)    B (1)
- & : G   B
- 2 & : G   B
- 3 & : G   B
- 4 & : G   B

**Measure 7**
- 1 & : G   B
- 2 & : G   B
- 3 & : G   B
- 4 & : G   B

**Measure 8**
- Beat 1: · · · · E (3) · · · · · · · · · · · · · · · E (1) · · · · · · · · · · · · · · · · · E (4) · · G (2)    B (1)
- & : G   B
- 2 & : G   B
- 3 & : G   B
- 4 & : G   B

**Measure 9**
- 1 & : G   B
- 2 & : G   B
- 3 & : G   B
- 4 & : G   B

# Metamorphosis One

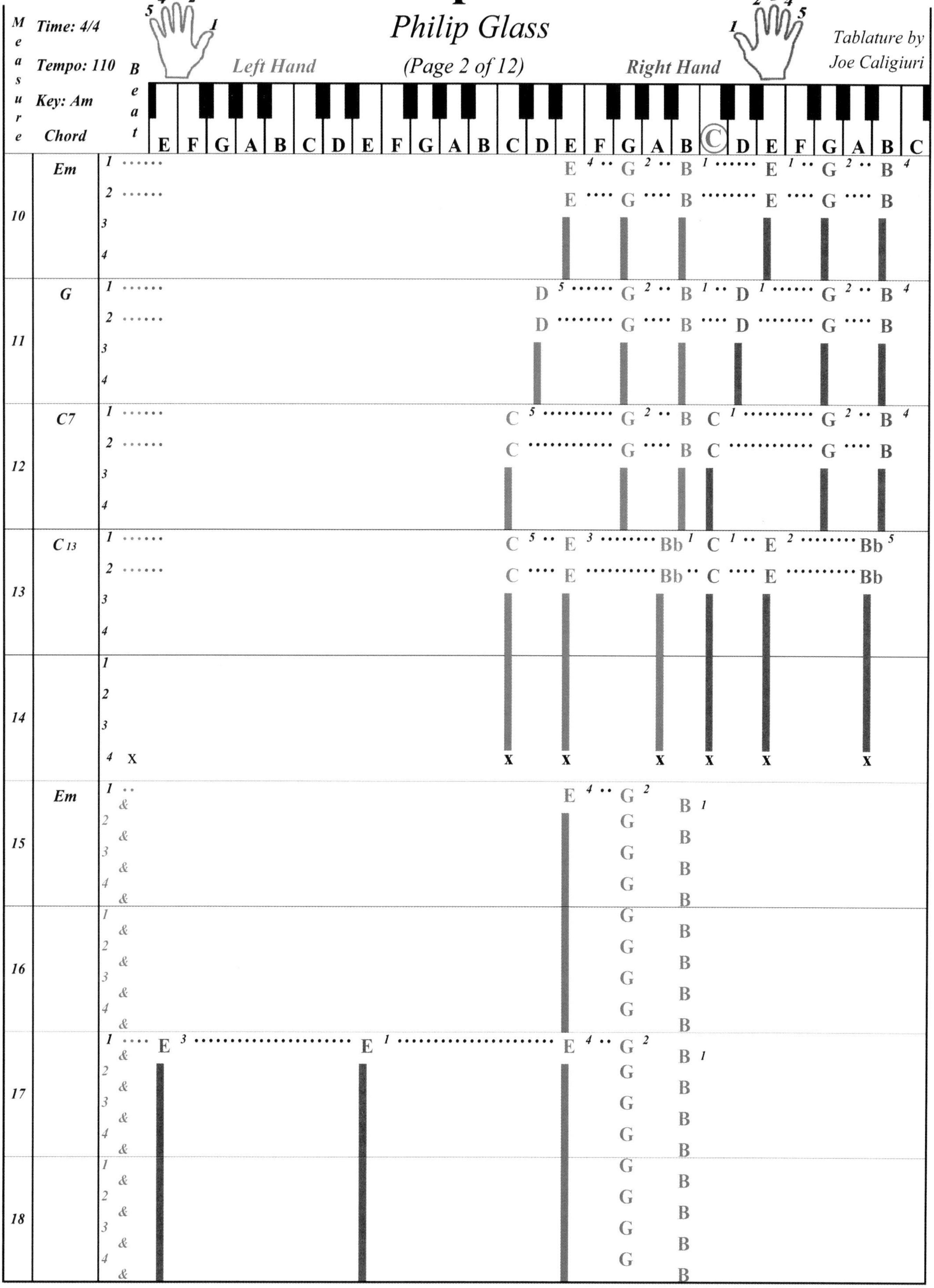

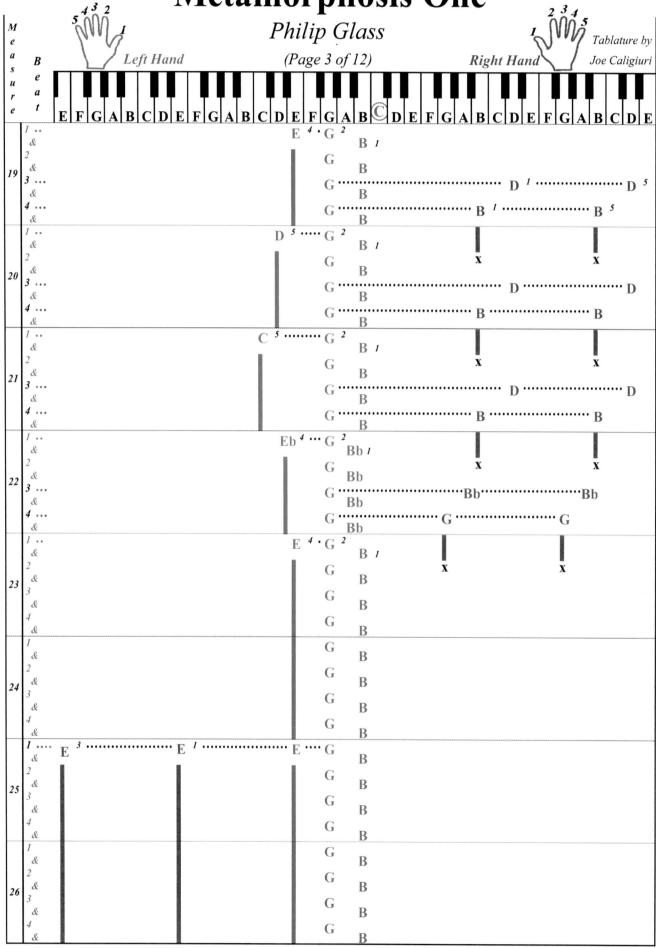

Metamorphosis One

*Philip Glass*

(Page 4 of 12)

Left Hand — Right Hand

Tablature by Joe Caligiuri

# Metamorphosis One

## *Philip Glass*

*Left Hand*

*Right Hand*

Tablature by
*Joe Caligiuri*

# Metamorphosis One

*Philip Glass*

*(Page 6 of 12)*

*Tablature by Joe Caligiuri*

*Time: 4/4*

*Tempo: 110*

*Key: Am*

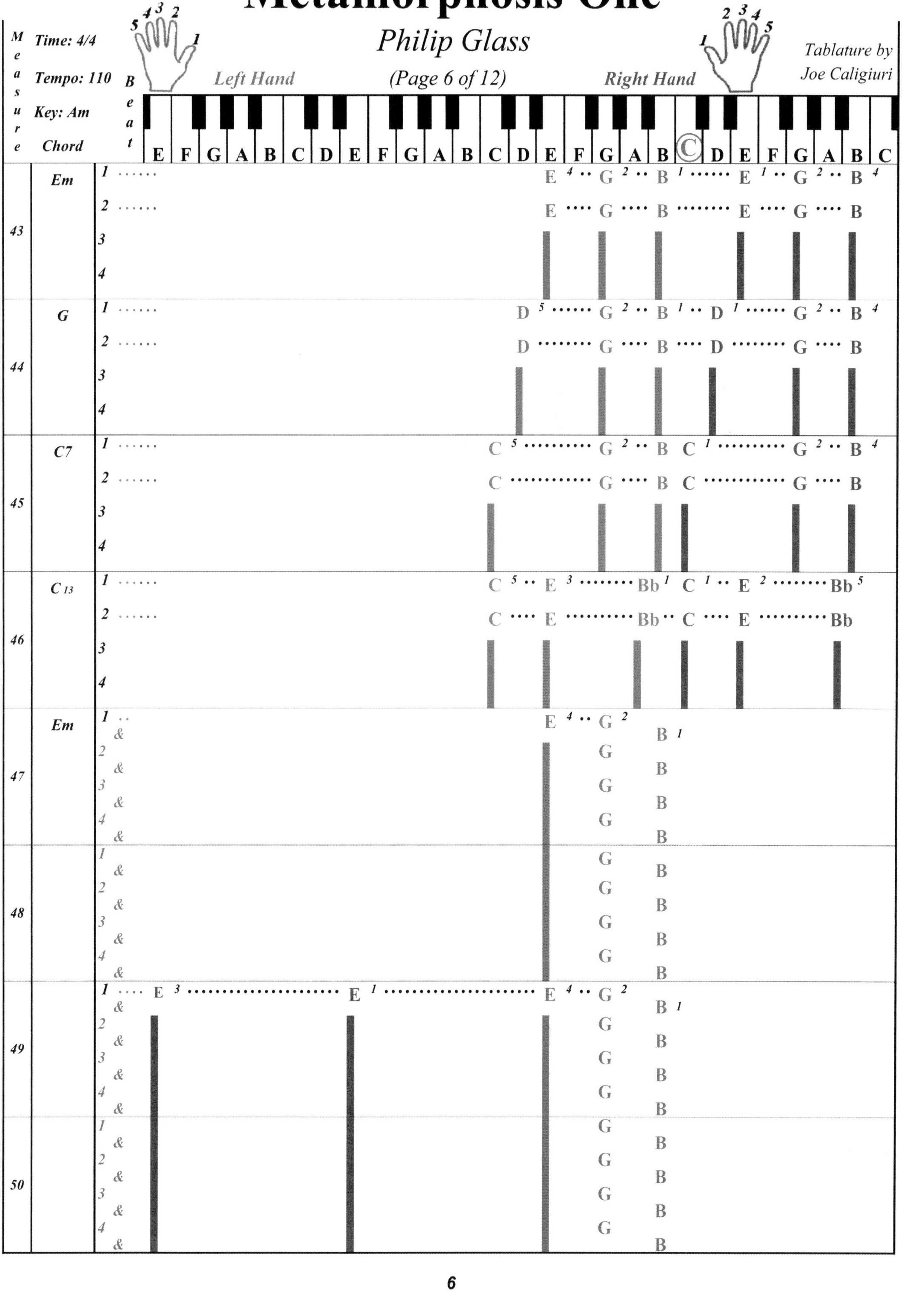

# Metamorphosis One

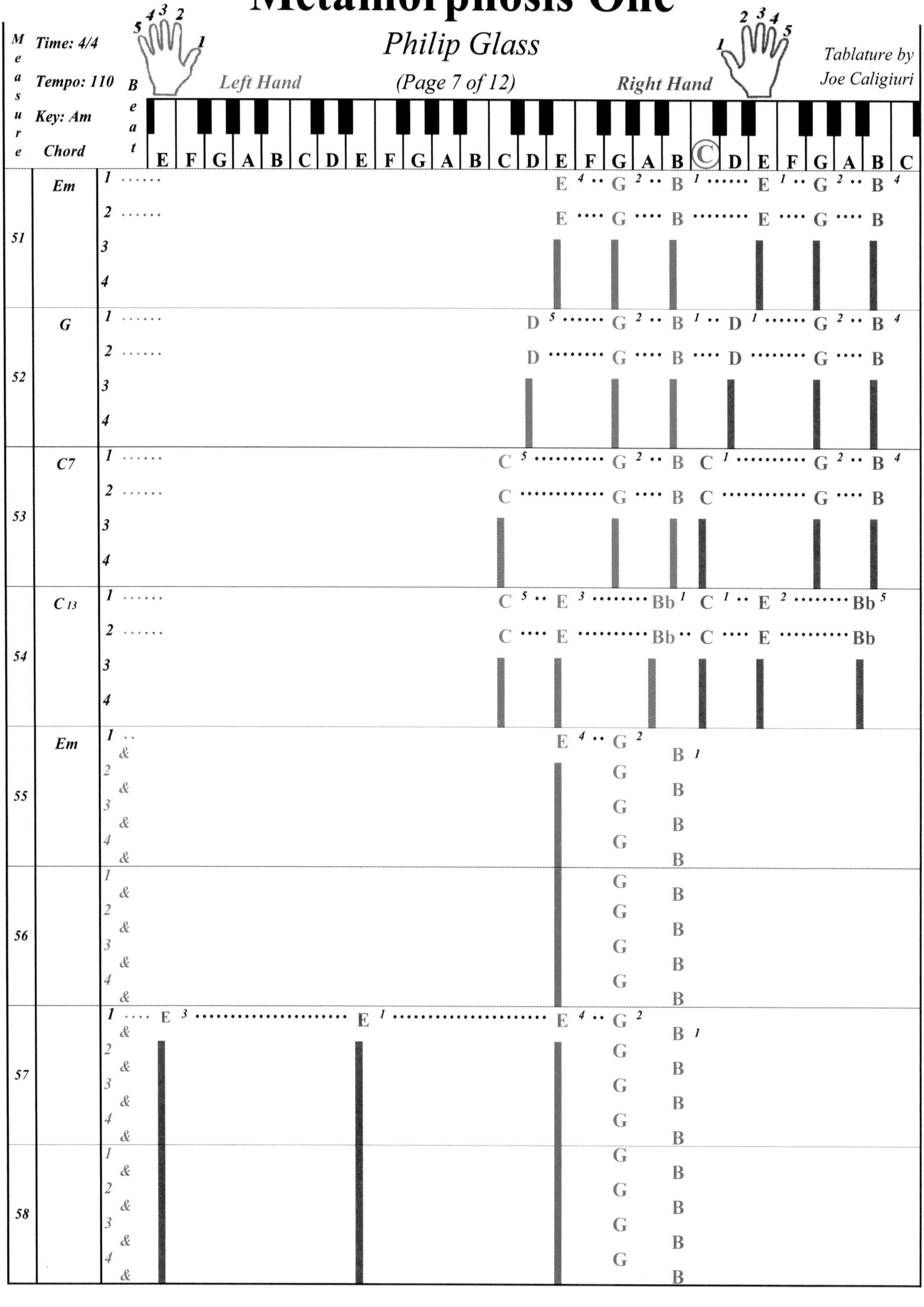

*Play Measures (59 - 66) 3 times*

8

# Metamorphosis One

## Philip Glass

Repeat Measures (67 - 74)

9

# Metamorphosis One

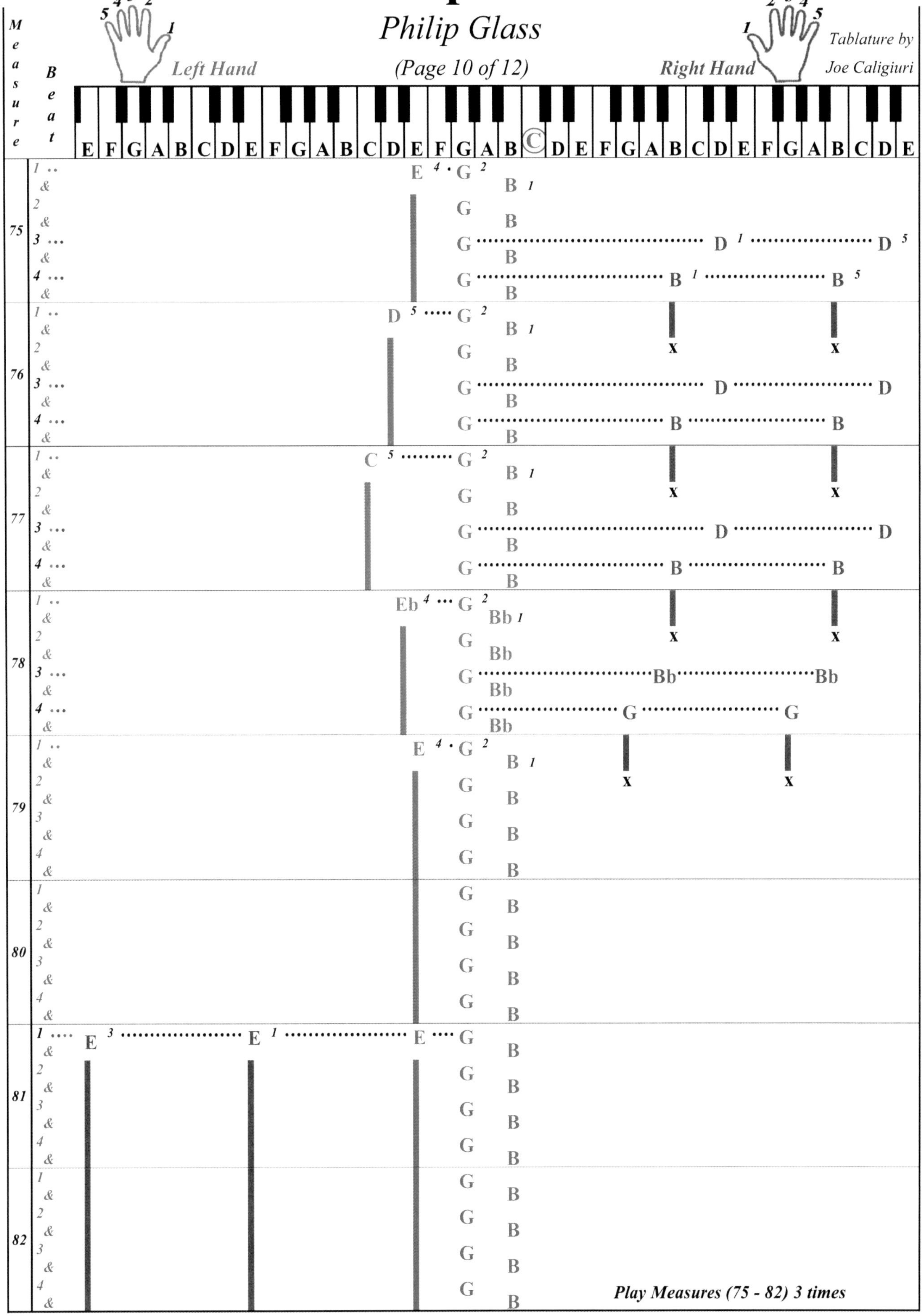

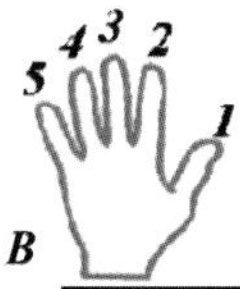

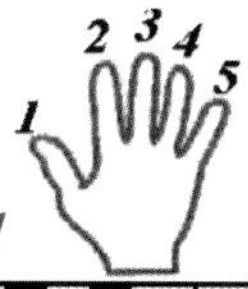

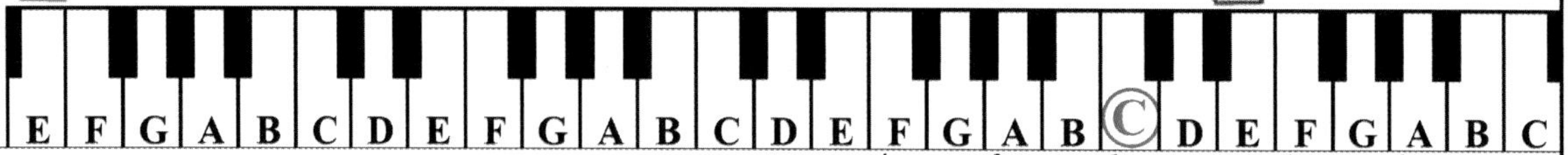

# Metamorphosis One

*Philip Glass*

Tablature by Joe Caligiuri

Time: 4/4
Tempo: 110
Key: Am

Left Hand — Right Hand

# Metamorphosis Two

## Philip Glass

*(Page 1 of 18)*

Tablature by
Joe Caligiuri

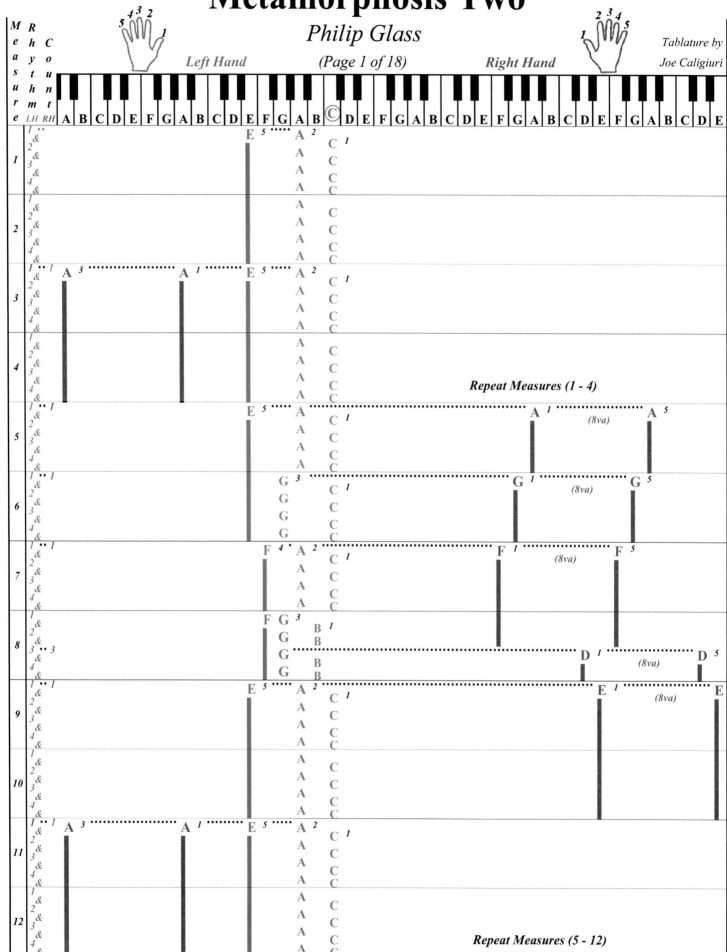

Repeat Measures (1 - 4)

Repeat Measures (5 - 12)

13

Left Hand   Right Hand

Tablature by Joe Caligiuri

Repeat (13 - 16)

Repeat Measures (21 - 24)
and Measures (21 & 22)
go to Measure 25

# Metamorphosis Two
## Philip Glass
### (Page 3 of 18)

Left Hand — Right Hand

Tablature by Joe Caligiuri

Repeat (25 - 28)

Repeat Measures (33 - 36)
and Measures (33 & 34)
go to Measure 37

15

# Metamorphosis Two

## Philip Glass

Left Hand — Right Hand

Tablature by Joe Caligiuri

Repeat Measures (37 - 40)

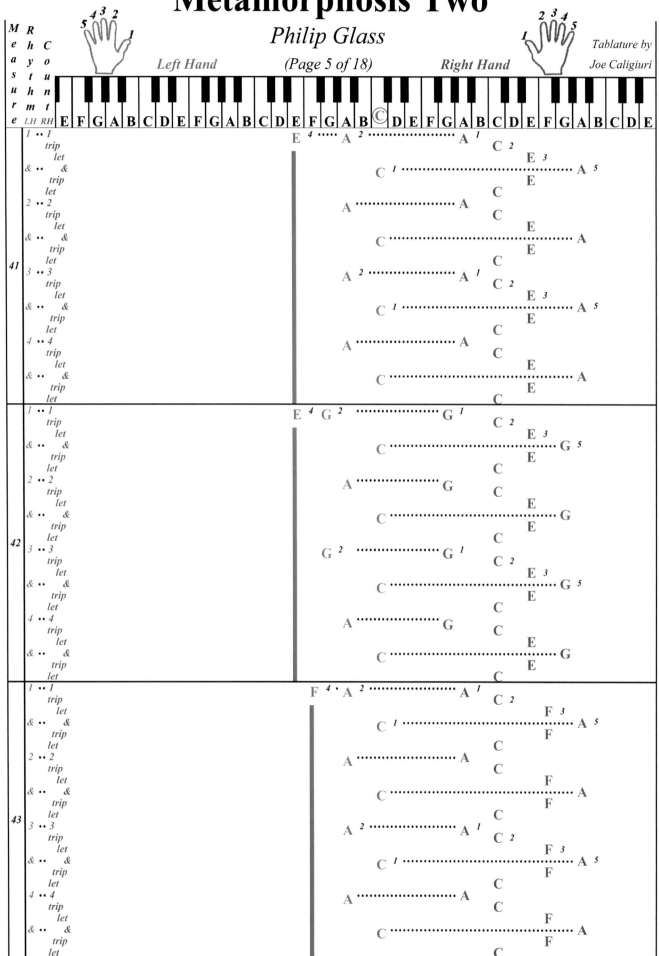

# Metamorphosis Two

## Philip Glass

*Left Hand*  (Page 6 of 18)  *Right Hand*

Tablature by Joe Caligiuri

18

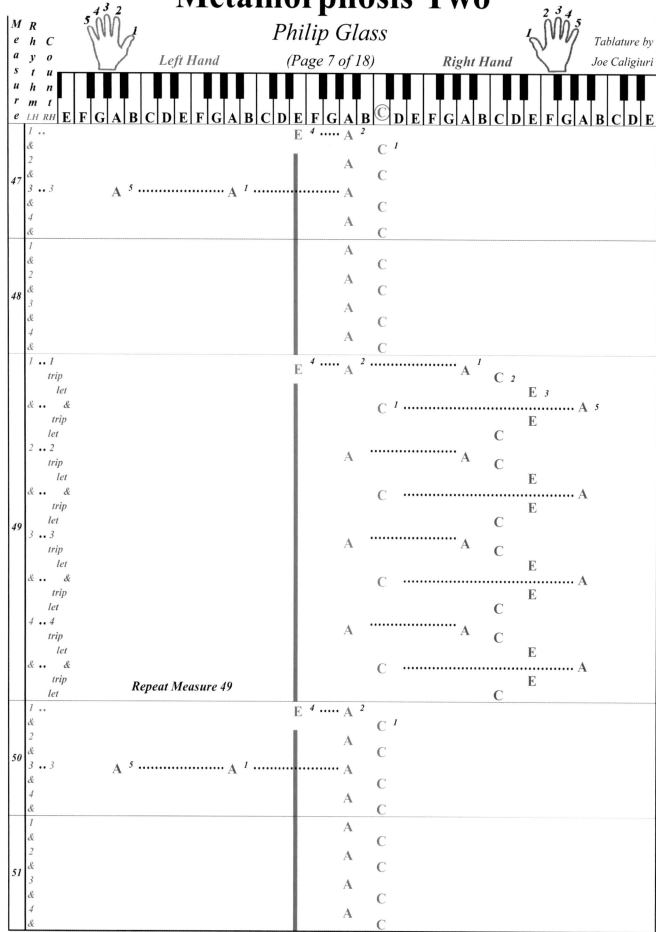

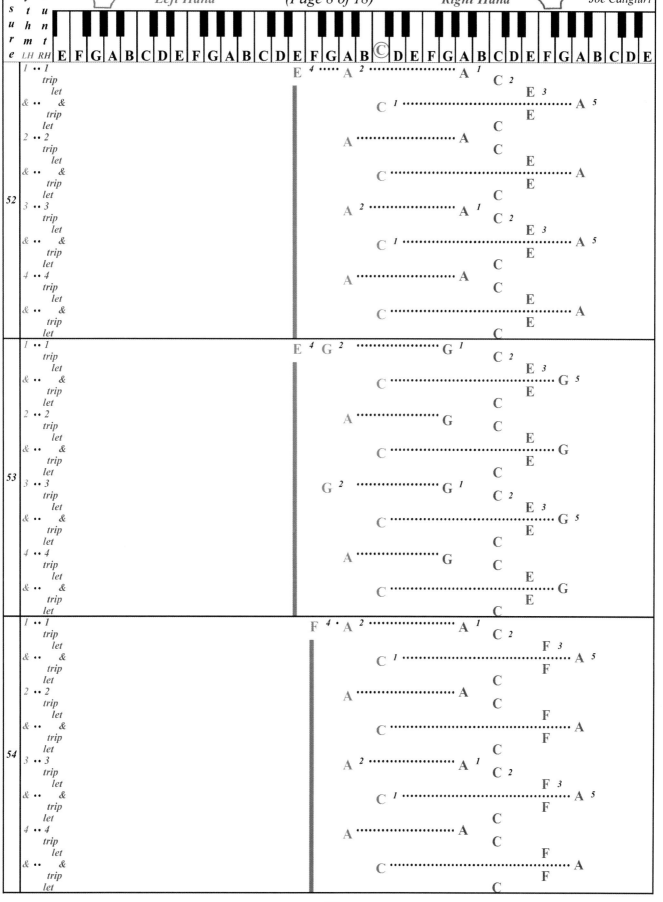

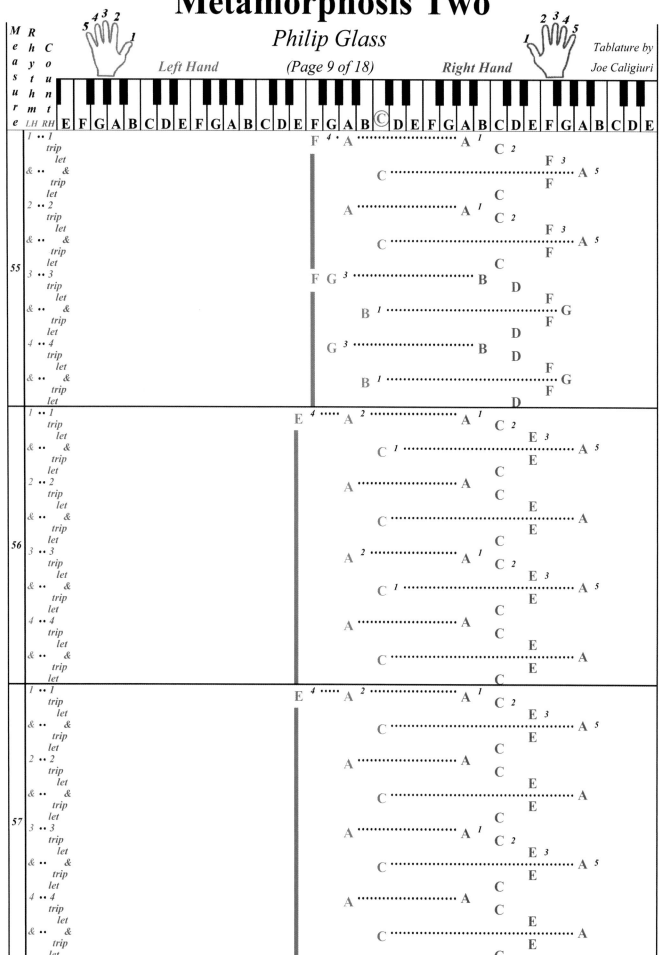

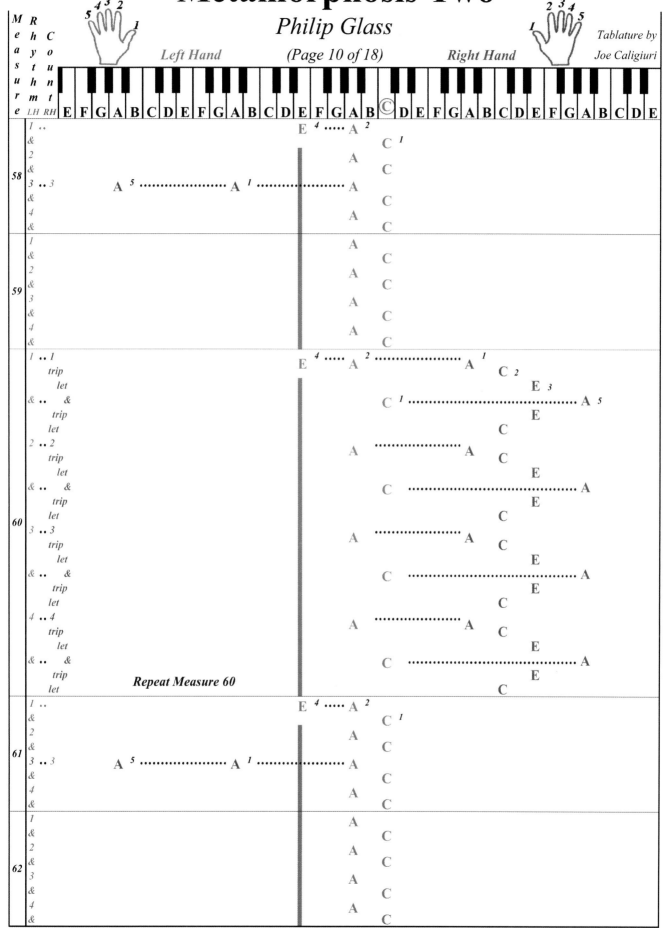

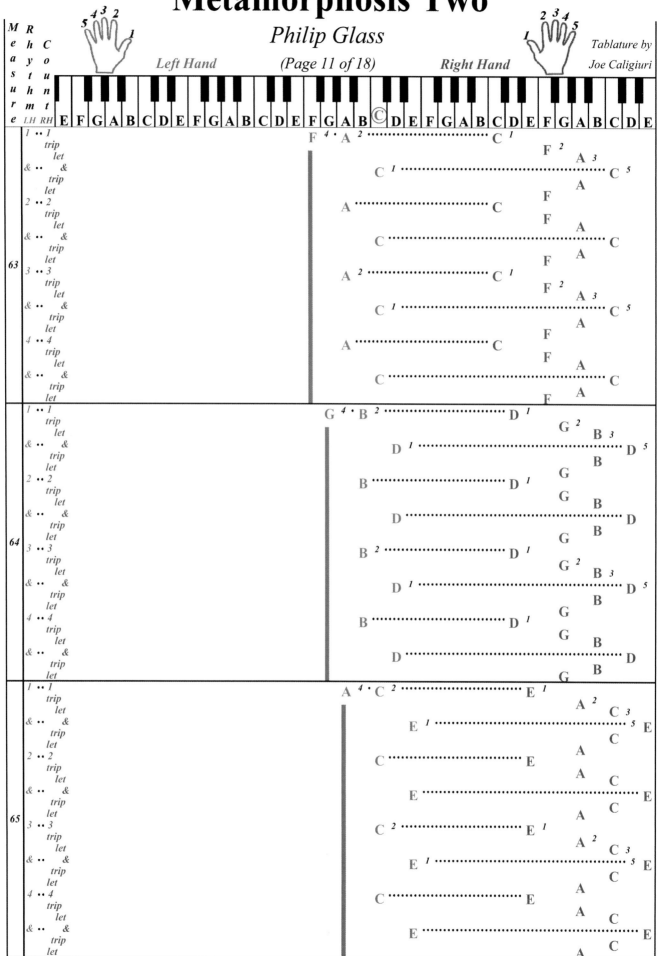

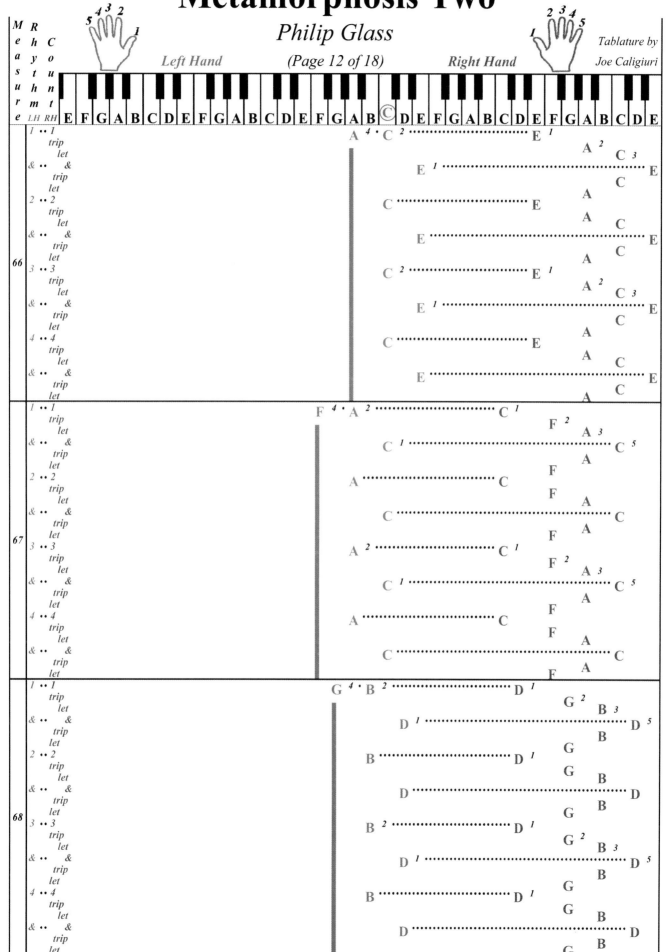

Left Hand    Right Hand

Tablature by Joe Caligiuri

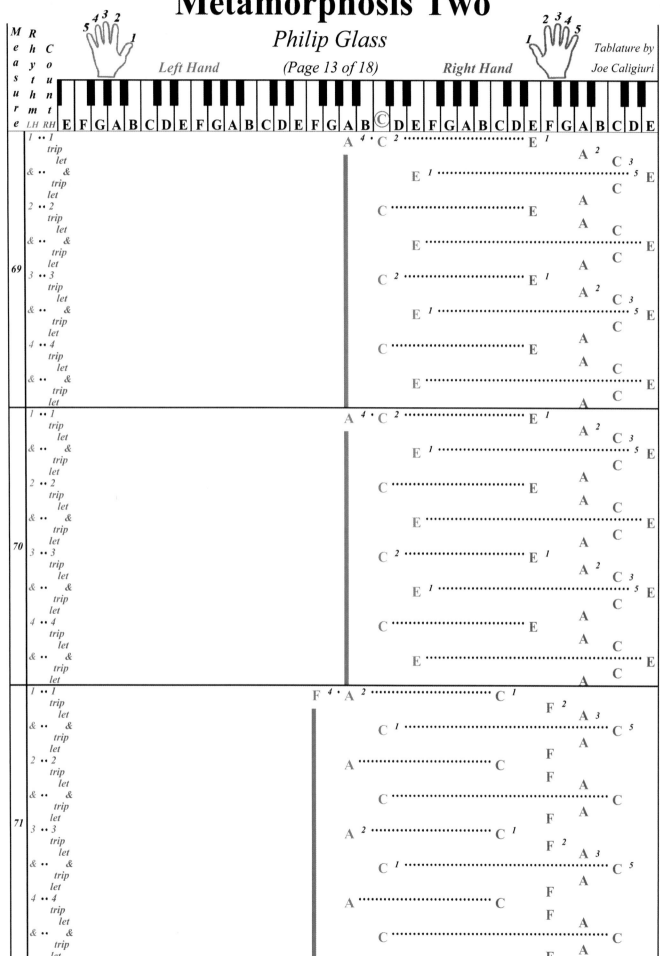

# Metamorphosis Two

*Philip Glass*

*(Page 14 of 18)*

*Left Hand* *Right Hand*

*Tablature by Joe Caligiuri*

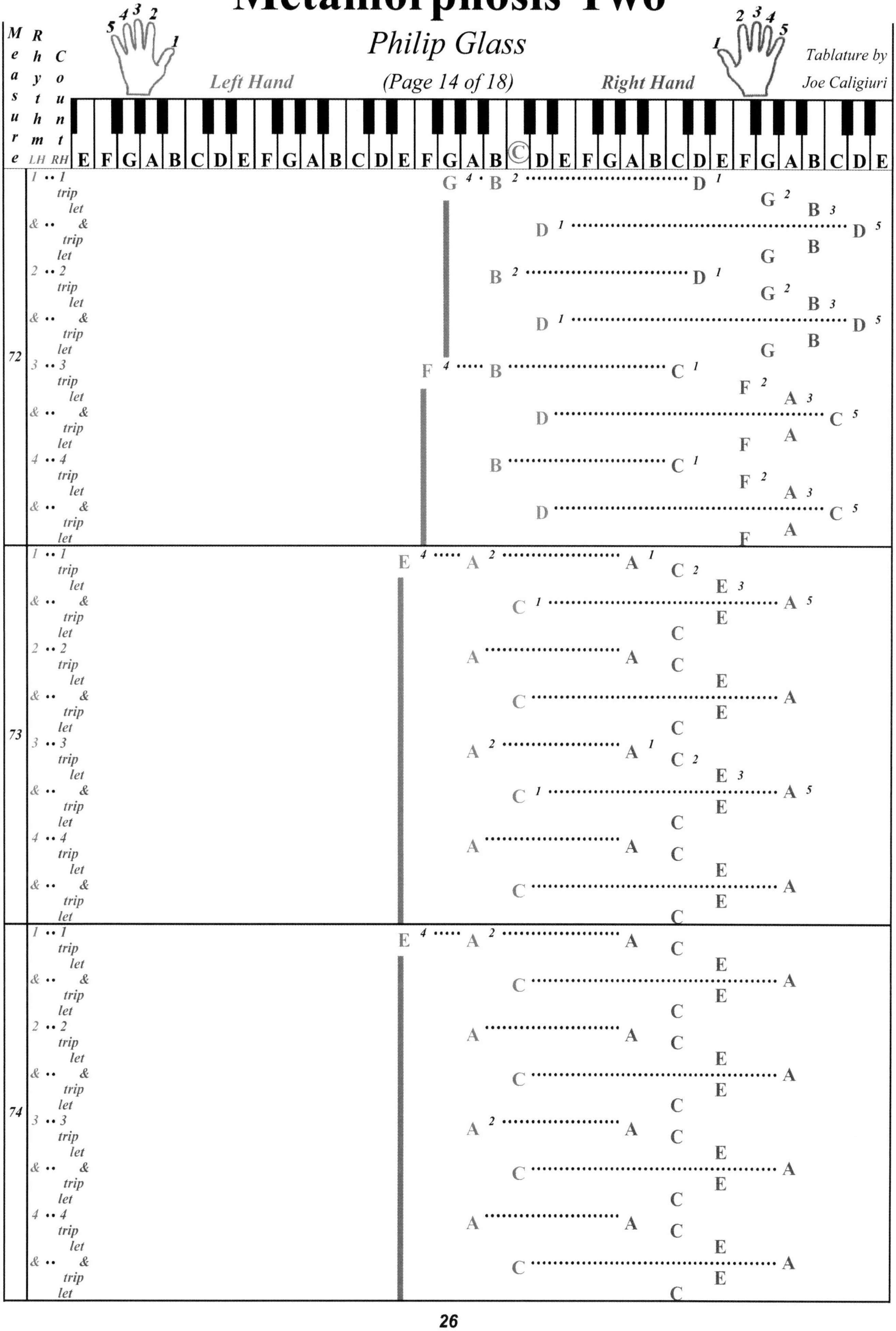

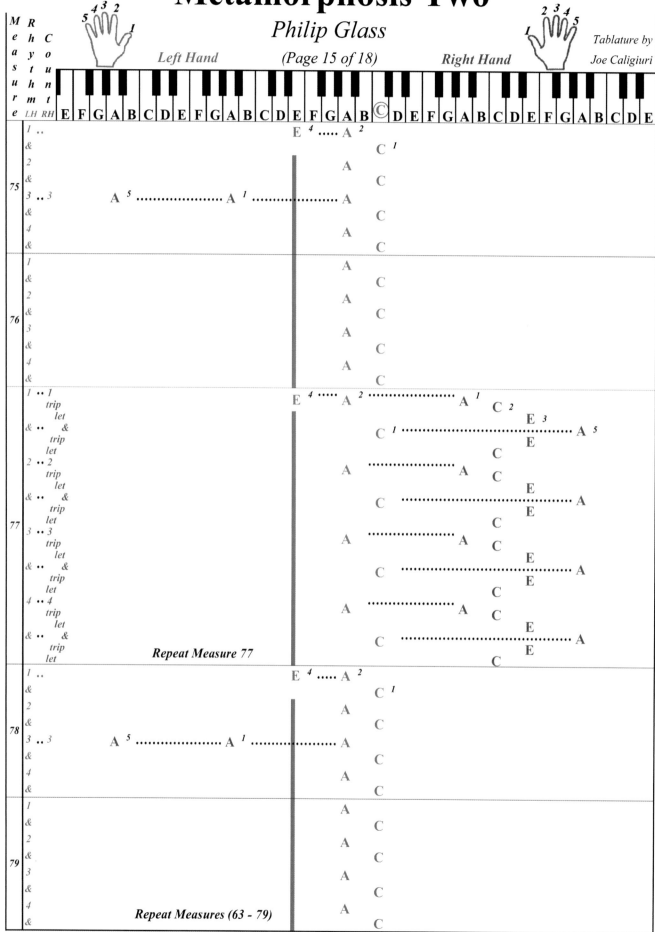

*Tablature by Joe Caligiuri*

*Repeat Measures (80 - 83)*

*(8va)*

*Repeat Measures (84 - 91)*

# Metamorphosis Two
## Philip Glass

*Tablature by Joe Caligiuri*

Left Hand     Right Hand

Repeat (92 - 95)

Repeat (100 & 101)
go to Measure 104

# Metamorphosis Two

*Philip Glass*

*Left Hand*　　*Right Hand*

*Tablature by Joe Caligiuri*

Repeat (104 - 107)

Repeat (112 & 113)
End on Measure 113

Made in the USA
San Bernardino, CA
21 February 2020